Power Exchange Magazine

POWER EXCHANGE

Issue 10

Published by
The Nazca Plains Corporation
PO Box 27432
Austin, TX 78755

Publisher	Robert Steele
Editor Emeritus	Robert J. Rubel , PhD
Editor	Richard Wagner, PhD
Copy Editor	Kavi Kardos
Art Director	Blake Stephens

Columnist

Anny Bryne

Robert Rubel, PhD

Richard Wagner, PhD, ACS

Robert Ritchey

Open Positions – Please Apply
Circulation Manager
Advertising Manager
Subscriptions Manager
Assistant to the Editor

Editorial, Volume 10

Lead, Follow, *or* Get the Hell Out of the Way

With apologies to General George Patton, Ol' "Blood & Guts" for modifying and repurposing his memorable quote as he marched thru Germany, we'd like to welcome you to a much-expanded **Power Exchange Magazine**.

The Patton quote does clearly express our views as to why the Nazca Plains Corporation has elected to revive Power Exchange Magazine. Over the last few years, while our magazine was on hiatus, we discovered to our great dismay, that no one else was willing or able to step up to fill the void. While there has been a proliferation of websites of dubious quality and intent nothing has come close to Power Exchange Magazine's stature as the preeminent alt culture forum for views about the fetish community and life on the sexual fringe.

We recommit ourselves to bring you fresh new voices that deserve your attention. People thinking outside the proverbial box about what is happening and what ought to be happening in our community at large. Of course we will also be featuring the views of people you've come to trust, stalwarts if you will, who have, with each passing year, cast a critical eye on who we are, how we are expressing ourselves, and the paths we chose to trod. In each of our upcoming issues you will be treated to an array of features found nowhere else.

- Timely book reviews calling your attention to authors of note.

- Insightful interviews with the movers and shakers of the new wave in alt culture.

- Thought-provoking imagery from artists and photographers on the cutting edge.

- Tantalizing erotica.

- Playful toy and product reviews.

- Club, dungeon, and play space reviews.

- And, of course, our famous lists — lists of distinguished presenters and alt culture events that are worthy of your attention.

Don't look for us to rubber stamp the drivel that passes for reviews and commentary in other places. Our staff, along with some very savvy industry insiders, will provide you with a provocative, no-hold-bared rating system on all things alt culture. You'll know precisely what's hot and what's not, what's worthy of your support and what's not. Sure, it'll be our opinion. And we make no apologies for that. I mean, isn't that what you look for in a resource that has traditionally stood apart from all the rest?

Toes will be stepped on, icons will be toppled, sacred cows will be slaughtered, and when the emperor has no clothes, we'll not shirk our duty to point that out. We look forward to a lively debate with you our readers. We encourage your thoughts, comments, and feedback (Editor@ PowerExchangeMagazine.com). If you have a bone to pick, we want to hear from you. If you have suggestion for one or another of our lists, we want to hear from you. If you've attended a helpful workshop or presentation, we want to hear from you. And if you think we should go fuck ourselves, we want to hear that too. But regardless of your tenor of your comments be person enough to speak your mind as somebody, not some anonymous douche.

Yes, we have a mission and we know what that mission is. We share General Patton's signature gruff conviction. We intend to lead. You looked to us for leadership in the past, and we step up to that again now. We encourage you to join us on the cutting edge; we want you to consider Power Exchange Magazine to be *your* magazine. Your contributions are always welcome. And if following is all you can do at the moment, we're cool with that too. What we won't abide is obstruction, there's way too much of that going on in the community as it is. Stand out of the way if you can't help your community move forward.

By this time next year, we hope you will be able to say of us that, while we may not have always shared your opinion, we did not duck the lead, nor did we shrink to follow, and we certainly never got in the way.

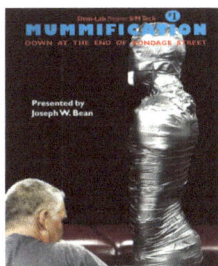
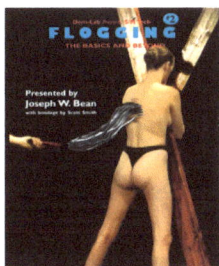
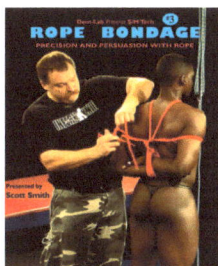
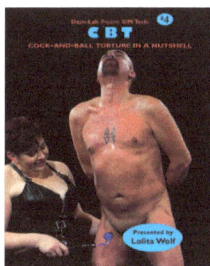
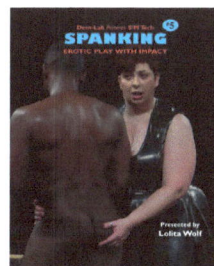
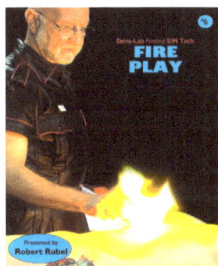
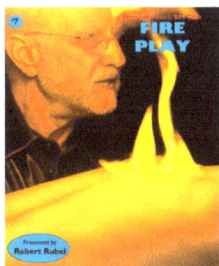
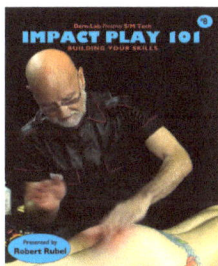
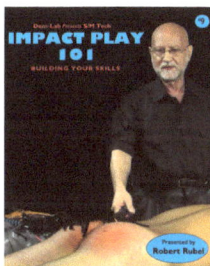
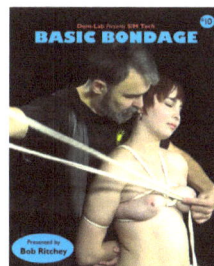
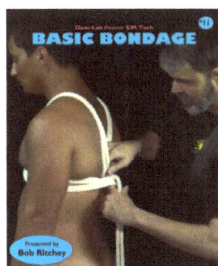
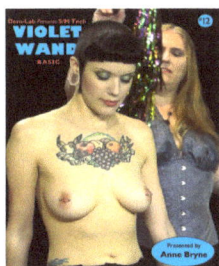
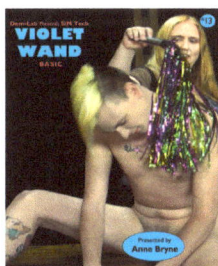
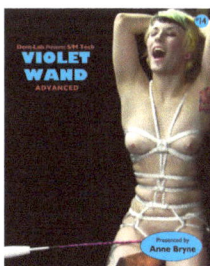
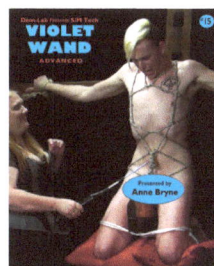

By Captain Ozgood-Feelgood

Interview
with Dr. Richard Wagner

Author of *The Gospel of Kink: A Modern Guide to Asking for What You Want and Getting What You Ask For.*

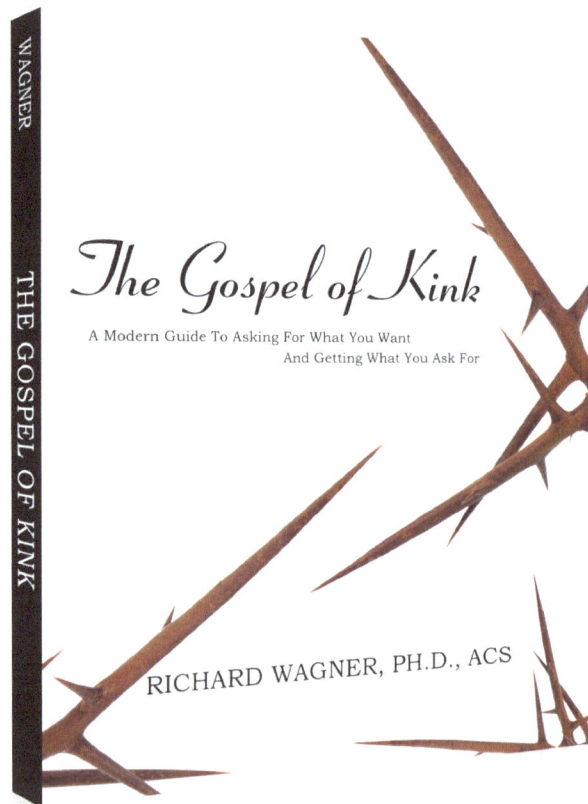

Richard Wagner, M.Div., Ph.D., ACS (also known affectionately as Dr. Dick) is a psychotherapist and clinical sexologist in private practice in Seattle. Dr. Wagner has been a practitioner of sex therapy and relationship counseling for over 30 years. His online sex advice column, which he has written for well over 15 years, can be found at drdicksexadvice.com.

CO-F: Welcome, Dr. Wagner – or should I say, Dr. Dick.

Congratulations on the publication of your new book, *The Gospel of Kink*. That's a pretty provocative title. I guess you like being inflammatory.

DD: Thank you. I do respond very well to Dr. Dick.

Yes, I like being provocative. But that's not why I chose *The Gospel of Kink* as this new book's title. Rather, I wanted to make a good news declaration, and this title fit the bill.

Anyone with a lick of religious upbringing, at least in the Christian tradition, will know that the word *gospel* means good news or glad tidings. This book is the culmination of 30-plus years of preaching the good news of the sex-positive and kink-aware movements, especially as it applies to those of us on the sexual fringe.

CO-F: You have quite a colorful past. Give us a thumbnail sketch of how you became Dr. Dick.

DD: I came to this work in a most unorthodox fashion. I was a Catholic priest for 20 years. I am the only Catholic priest in the world with a doctorate in clinical sexology. I completed my post-graduate work with the publication of my doctoral thesis concerning the sexual attitudes and behaviors of gay Catholic priests in the active ministry in 1981. This was unprecedented research back then (and still is now, for that matter).

Soon thereafter, there was a firestorm of international publicity. I became known as the "Gay Priest," as if I was the only one. Needless to say, this notoriety (some say infamy) effectively ended my priesthood. Despite fighting the Vatican for the next 13 years, in an attempt to salvage my ministry,

> You went from priest to pornographer in one fell swoop?

the deed was done. I was dismissed from my religious community, and while I am technically still a priest, I do not practice as such anymore.

My career as a therapist in San Francisco coincided with the advent of HIV/AIDS in the early '80s. Not surprisingly, my practice evolved into working primarily with sick and dying people. In the mid-'90s I founded a nonprofit organization called PARADIGM, Enhancing Life Near Death. It was an outreach program for terminally ill, chronically ill, elder and dying people. This was brilliant, cutting-edge work, but alas, I couldn't find the funding to continue. The end

of that program precipitated a rather sudden move to Seattle in 1999.

CO-F: Were you writing the Dr. Dick column before you moved to Seattle?

DD: I was. The column's humble beginning was with gay.com, when that website was a hole-in-the wall outfit in the South of Market neighborhood of San Francisco.

I continued to work with the sick and dying after moving to Seattle. I developed programming for women who were newly diagnosed with ovarian cancer and men with prostate cancer. I wanted to create a video series for people experiencing life threatening and/or disfiguring illnesses to help them deal with reintegrating sex and intimacy into their lives post-diagnosis, and I soon realized that I would need to fund this project on my own because no mainstream, disease-based foundation would touch the issue of sex. Faced with how I might do that, friends prevailed on me to start by shooting porn. Thus my video production company, Daddy Oohhh! Productions, was born.

CO-F: You went from priest to pornographer in one fell swoop?

DD: Precisely. The lure of money to fund my greatest passion is what attracted me to the venture. Unfortunately, that load of money never materialized. But while I was shooting porn, my interest was to create projects that were different in style and tone from what ruled the marketplace at the time.

CO-F: The tagline for your column is "Sex Advice with an Edge." What gives your column its edge? How is it different from other sex advice columns?

DD: I focus on human sexuality particularly as it intersects with art, religion, popular culture, relationships, our health and wellbeing, entertainment, shopping and politics. None of my professional peers take so wide an aim.

As one would guess, I respond to questions submitted to me online, and I offer my advice in written form as well as via podcast. My site is peppered with provocative imagery. I do not shy away from sexually explicit photos. This is a big no-no for other professional advice sites.

I like to chat with interesting and controversial guests – authors, artists, sex workers, pundits and porn stars. I investigate the sexual underground and present interviews with fascinating people on the cutting edge of the sex-positive and kink-aware world. The Dr. Dick Review Crew and I also review adult products at drdicksextoyreviews.com.

I offer tips to my audience on staying healthy, enriching their sex lives and growing their relationships, and I try to do it all with a sense of humor.

CO-F: Your latest book, *The Gospel of Kink*, marks a significant departure from your earlier books. You're entering a field that, some would say, is super saturated with self-help books. What makes yours stand out?

DD: For starters, it's a workbook. It's actually a workshop in book form. You're right that there are a lot of self-help books out there targeted at kinksters, but I can safely say that *The Gospel of Kink* is fundamentally different in style and scope from everything else I've ever read on the topic.

> The Gospel of Kink is fundamentally different in style and scope from everything else I've ever read on the topic.

My book offers readers an interactive way to access information, explore feelings and learn from their peers in the alt culture, as well as a safe and secure place to air their concerns without fear of being judged for their lifestyle choices. Readers get an opportunity to confront their relationship concerns in a really adventurous way. Basically, they become members of an on-the-page workshop.

CO-F: So, practically, how does that work?

DD: Each of the four chapters involves readers in the workshop process. They get to know and identify with the issues and concerns of the other workshop participants, who I write about in the book, and involve themselves in all the discussions and exercises.

This workshop-in-a-book format also gives readers access to a panel of skilled practitioners who offer valuable information on timely issues like communication, power exchange, polyamory, jealousy, sex and intimacy, relationship building and conflict resolution.

CO-F: That sounds like a relatively cutting-edge approach.

DD: Yeah, I figured if I was going to add something to the existing body of work, some of which is amazingly good, I would need to make my contribution unique. It would need to stand out, or else I'd have to just forget about the whole thing.

The best part of *The Gospel of Kink* is that it's not a one-size-fits-all sort of thing. Readers are encouraged to design their own practical solutions to the unique alt-cultural issues they face. The workbook will help them develop a strategy for navigating the relationship pitfalls and communication dead-ends that so often plague those of us on the sexual fringe.

CO-F: The book is based on a face-to-face workshop that you provide in Seattle. Why the need for a book version?

DD: The face-to-face workshop only reaches a tiny fraction of the people I can serve with a book. It's the same reason I have an online presence as Dr. Dick – that presence serves people all over the world, not just those who can connect with me in person through my private practice. I'm hoping *The Gospel of Kink* will enjoy the same kind of success and will reach those who need this information, but who are unable or hesitant to connect with their alt-culture peers.

CO-F: Well, we wish you the best of luck with the book and hope to meet you in person someday – I suppose you will be taking *The Gospel of Kink* on the road?

DD: I hope so. The many alt-culture conferences, retreats and workshops across the country and abroad are perfect opportunities for appearances and book signings, not to mention general proselytizing. I still have a way to go in spreading *The Gospel of Kink*.

Captain Ozgood-Feelgood is a card-carrying kinkster, renowned troublemaker, sometimes blogger, reader of more than one book and long-time resident of San Francisco. He is a frequent contributor of book reviews and author interviews to *Power Exchange* and other publications.

Column by Anne Bryne

Toy Bag

Tips and Tricks

Are you curious about how to fit a gag into your bag, or about the differences between strap-on designs? Have you seen something used at a party or a demo and don't know where to find it, or exactly what it is? This is the place to look for those answers.

Much is written and available concerning how to use the various toys and devices that bring such joy to us all. Whether you're into singletails, paddles, floggers, the sensuous feel of rope, fire, wax, electricity or the beloved Hitachi vibrator, it's possible to find classes, online resources or entire conventions to help you learn more about your chosen passion. This column has a different focus. We'll discuss what to look for when you buy your implement and how to care for your new acquisition once you get it home. Occasionally, we will even suggest online shops or trade shows where you might find it.

Future issues will address lotions and potions, kilts and corsets, leather of all sorts and storage containers and carriers, to name a few.

While the tools are fun, it's nice to remember that each of us already has that one magical implement that fosters the creation of the "perfect scene." What is this perfect item that will thrill you beyond your wildest desires? It's you. Without a doubt, what each of us brings to the table has more impact than anything else when we seek to create those special moments and connections with our partners. What are you bringing to your table?

Glans Ring - Penis Plug

This little device is really fun to wear and use. A great beginner's piece for getting comfortable with wearing a ring and the feeling of having something penetrating your urethra. It's so comfortable, making it perfect for all-day and/or all-night wear. This will definitely launch the interest in going to the next step for something that reaches a little deeper. This penis jewelry piece is totally made out of 316LVM Surgical Steel. Offering men a much cooler way to stop the influx. This is a penis jewelry piece that will definitely become your favorite. Along with being functional, the glans ring promises pleasure too.

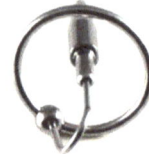

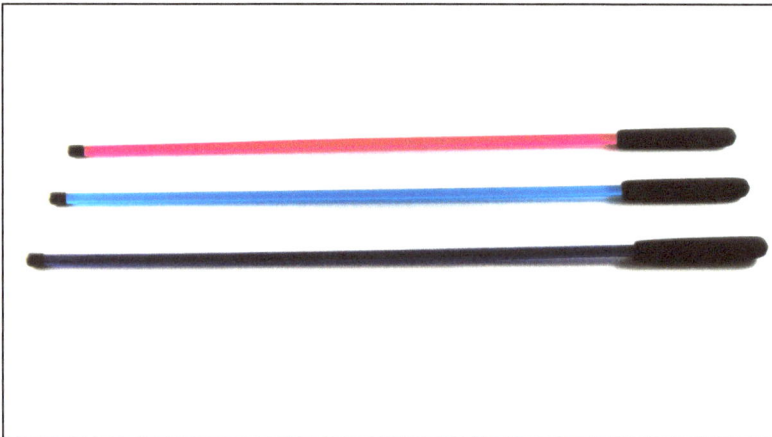

Acrylic Rods

Impact toys come in all sorts of flavors. Rods are items that look like canes but are of a manmade material. Cheap and easy to replace if they break, acrylic rods can be a great introduction to the world of caning and discipline.

Adjustable Tit Clamps with Chain

Add some spice to your life with these silver beaded Nipple Clamps from California Exotic. Strikingly sexy beaded chain design. Comfortable rubber coated clamps are non-tarnishing have incredible holding power. Stimulating clamps are great for teasing your nipples alone or with the one you want to dominate. Totally adjustable, clamps tighten and release with a twist of the screws. Sturdy clamps are connected by an elegant 13 inch beaded chain. Stylish, arousing, and easy to use. Clamp up your night and have some real fun.

Huggers

Finally, a way for men and women to enjoy nipple piercings without being pierced is here. The Huggers are small, stylish, round earth magnets with the power to put - and stay put - with two degrees of force. The smaller Huggers pinch lightly and look great on men and women. The large Huggers are a force to be reckoned with, pinching harder and useful even through several inches of flesh; no need for that Glans ring anymore! This set comes with two pairs of small and one pair of large Huggers. Geared more for guys, the small Huggers are for the nipples, and the large Huggers are bound for the Glans area. Caution: Care must be used when applying AND removing the Huggers, as these very strong magnets can "leap" together and cause bruising, chafing, and other minor injuries. For external use only.

Ball Gag

The ball gag is a fixture of the BDSM or Power Exchange lifestyle. Sometimes you just don't want to hear anything further from your partner! This ball gag incorporates the classic 1 2/3" ball with a strap of leather that has been inserted into a fitted slot in the ball. The ball fits all the way into the mouth. For added safety, it has holes for ease of breathing.

The toys on these pages are available from www.altsitesltd.com.

Column by Robert Rubel

On *Assumptions*: Some Gentle Warnings

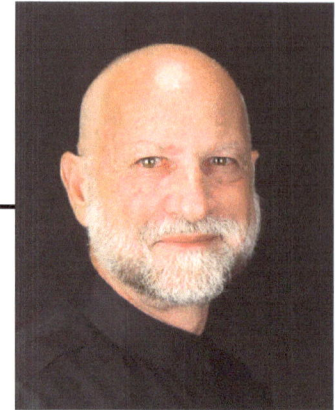

"I Met a Master Online...": On Titles and Such

The Internet world is unlike the real world when it comes to Masters, Mistresses, Doms, Dommes and slaves. The way these words are used on the Internet often sets up expectations that are wildly different than what these words mean to experienced BDSMers. You can easily be misled. On the Internet, anyone can be anything and call themselves whatever they wish. It's a bit more complicated than that in real time—but *real time* definitions of titles are also caught up in controversy and differing opinions.

Perhaps the most controversial title surrounds the word "master", as it has multiple meanings in English. It can mean someone who has "mastered" some field of study, (hence a "master mason" or a "master electrician") and thus represent a rank of recognition within a field. Alternatively, "master" can refer to someone who has power and authority over others (historically referring to servants or slaves).

Because the word "master" implies seniority combined with skill and experience, there is a (natural?) tendency for some BDSMers to proclaim themselves to be "Master ___" because… why not? There is no qualifying process to go through before you can use the title/rank.

As a self-bestowed descriptor, straights within the BDSM scene sometimes put the word "Master" before their name. In some cases, the title is warranted, for these are seriously senior BDSM practitioners who take their Master/slave responsibilities very seriously. However, in other cases, the title "Master" can be misleading: Some newcomers seem to employ the "Master" title as a way of giving the appearance that they are wise, mature, experienced, and trustworthy, while others (also new to this scene) mistakenly think

that a "Master" and a "Dom" are essentially different ends of a sliding scale of authority and they want to be recognized as being a *serious Dom.*

The trouble is, anyone can call himself anything. This differences in meaning can cause some problems for those new to BDSM who are likely to assume that because a person is called "Master So-and-So" they *must* be senior (wise, trusted, experienced) in the community.

Don't place your trust in a title; check them out. Ask for references. The most worthy seldom refer to themselves as "Master;" they let others use that honorific.

ROBERT RUBEL IS ALSO THE AUTHOR OF:

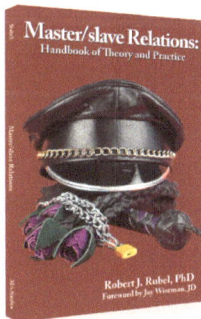

Master/slave Relations
Handbook of Theory and Practice

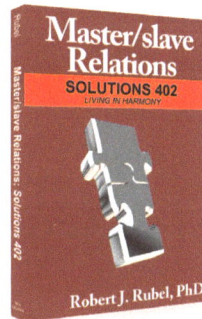

Master/slave Relations
Solutions 402:
Living in Harmony

Master/slave Relations
Communications 401:
The Advanced Course

Protocol Handbook for the Leather Slave
Theory and Practice

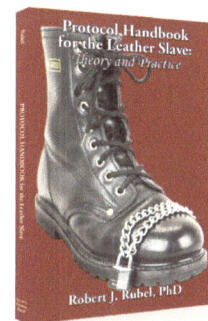

Sex Advice with an Edge with Dr. Dick

a *Kink*
in her *Pink*

Name: Dena
Gender: Female
Age: 32
Location: NYC

I love my cunt. In fact, you could say I have a cunt fetish. I love to stuff my cunt with really big toys. My current boyfriend introduced me to fist-fucking and I love it. I guess what I want to know is: Can this be dangerous?

I love it—a chick who refers to her pussy as a cunt! Own it, girl!

But what's this… you're just now gettin' around to askin' if fisting is dangerous? Not before, but *after* you've had a fist in your cunt? Well, so much for being proactive. I'd be willing to guess that you probably already have some data on the advisability of this form of extreme sex play. You certainly have enough information to declare that you *love it*.

Okay, for everyone else in my audience (both those with cunts and those who are cuntless) who haven't heard of fisting, let's start at the beginning. I trust everyone knows what fingering is, right? Whether it's fingerin' a pussy or an asshole, it's loads of fun to diddle someone's insides. We already know that fingering a dude's hole will stimulate his prostate, which more and more non-gay men are discovering to be way fun. And fingering a pussy can stimulate a lady's G-spot, which a lot of women find delightfully pleasurable. Okay, sex fans, take fingering and multiply that by five. That's right—fisting is inserting a whole hand/fist into a cunt or asshole.

> I hasten to add that gettin' a whole fist inside a pussy is somewhat easier than gettin' a fist in an asshole.

For all you folks who haven't fainted away, yes, it is anatomically possible, and yes, it can be *extremely* pleasurable. I hasten to add that gettin' a whole fist inside a pussy is somewhat easier than gettin' a fist in an asshole. But for folks like you, Dena—those who are into massive penetration—nothing is a bigger turn-on.

To your question: Is this practice harmful? Well, not if you do it right. First off, the fisting Top does *not* make a fist and ram it home.

Fisting aficionados say that handballing is the most intimate and complete way to touch another human being, but this kind of extreme penetration has to be worked up to slowly and gently.

Trust and communication between partners are essential, as is tons of lube. Some folks swear by Crisco; others think the legendary J-Lube—a handy-dandy concentrate that veterinarians use—stands apart from the rest because it's the most slippery and gooey. If you choose this stuff, you simply follow the recipe for reconstituting the concentrate. Recipes are available on several handballing sites.

The fisting Top must, of course, respect his/her partner's limits and pain threshold. Safe fisting is happy fisting. And, to that end, Dena, tell your boyfriend to keep the following concerns in mind:

First of all, cut and file all your nails until every finger is as smooth as it can possibly be. Your fingers will be in some very delicate places—places that may not have pain receptors. You'll want to ensure that you minimize all chance of causing injury.

Make sure your partner is relaxed, comfortable and turned on. When a woman is aroused, her vagina relaxes, expands and lengthens—all very important for accommodating a fist, don't 'cha know.

Even the wettest cunt will need lots and lots of lube during fisting. There's no such thing as too much lube, so prepare for a big fat mess. Lube the palm of your hand, the back of your hand and between your fingers. Keep applying lube as you go. Push the lube into the pussy (or asshole) with your fingers. Remember, if you're using latex gloves, that oil-based lubricants dissolve latex.

Start with one or two fingers and work your way up to three and then four. Most people need some time to further relax their muscles, and some may require several stretching sessions, over weeks or even months, before they can actually accommodate a whole hand.

The Top must be sensitive to the bottom's feelings. You are trying to persuade part of her body to open for you and to admit part of your body deep inside her. If you take your time, the energy exchange between you and her will move you both into an altered state. Communication and relaxation are the keys.

Once you've reached a five-finger insertion, you're almost there. But it's at this precise point that the handballing Top needs to be the most attentive. Your partner's pussy is being stretched to its near limit. Your partner is going to be riding a wave of pain and pleasure. If you find her cunt has reached its limit for the time being, respect that and pull out slowly. But if your partner wants more, then slip your knuckles inside. Be sure to fold your thumb "inside" your fingers, so that

your hand will *naturally* form an elongated fist. Think of the shape of a duck's bill. This makes your hand into a wedge that allows you to gradually stretch your partner open as you press on. Apply steady but slow pressure.

> Even the wettest cunt will need lots and lots of lube during fisting. There's no such thing as too much lube, so prepare for a big fat mess."

Your partner should be telling you when to push and when to back off. Careless fisting can cause muscle and tissue injuries from the Top going too fast or too hard. Obviously, there's gonna be some discomfort during handballing. Listen to the owner of that pussy or ass; she or he will let you know the difference between *hurts so good* and *hurts real bad*.

The knuckles are the widest part of the hand and the most difficult part to get past the opening of the cunt. If there's gonna be resistance to the insertion of the fist, this is probably the point at which it will happen. Wait until your partner is ready before making the big push. She may be able to help by bearing down (as if she were giving birth or having a bowel movement). Once your knuckles slip past the ring of muscles around the vaginal entrance, the pressure will ease off. Now, *gently* roll your hand into a fist. I'll add another reminder here to keep those fingernails as short as possible—moving from the duck-bill shape to the balled fist can cause some extremely unfortunate scraping if you have any nails at all.

Once you've formed a fist, the owner of the pussy or asshole may want a gentle pumping movement. Fisting produces intense sensations that can be different for every bottom; so ask what feels good.

When the session is done, make your hand into the duck-bill wedge shape again and slide it out just as gently and slowly as it went in.

Good luck, and please continue to enjoy your cunt!

About Dr. Dick

Therapy, Counseling, Consulting, or Coaching sessions available by telephone, online, or in person. Contact Dr Dick through his site: drdicksexadvice.com

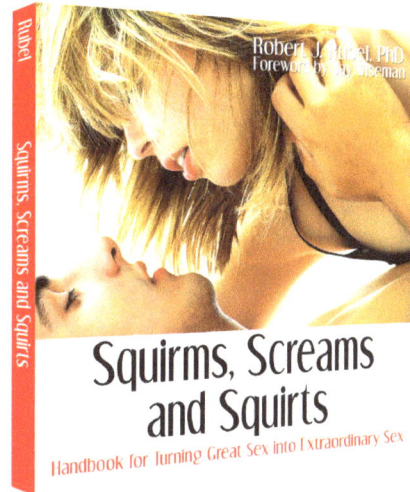

Squirms, Screams, and Squirts:
Handbook for Turning Great Sex into Extraordinary Sex

Not just another sex techniques book, this book includes lots of material about the psychological side of setting up an extraordinary sexual evening."

It's the difference between imitating great sex and creating it.

From great sex to extraordinary sex, Squirms, Screams and Squirts will take you there.

For the first time, an easily understood manual that demystifies some of the most complicated issues surrounding pleasing a lady.

• The Art and Science of Oral Sex
• Crystal Clear Descriptions of Female Anatomy
• Sex Toys and Precisely How to Use Them
• How to "Stair-Step" Sexual Pleasuring
• Enjoying Taboos and other Outrageous Concepts
• … and how to perform them safety.

Available at Amazon.com, Barnes & Noble, or your local bookstore.

By Staff Writer

Dungeon Review

The Sanctuary for Lifestyle Arts

Irving, Texas

If I hadn't known to look for it amidst the warehouses and industrial spaces, I would never have guessed that one of the best dens of iniquity was home to BDSM gatherings every weekend. The Sanctuary has been in operation for over a decade under the same management. There are groups that have been meeting there for that whole time. Sure, there have been groups that have folded, but others have risen to take their place. In spite of that, I'm somewhat amazed that the space is still open. If it wasn't for the determination and generosity of its owner, it wouldn't be. The dedication of the people that volunteer at the dungeon matches that of the owner, who makes this one of the friendliest venues I've encountered.

To get to the front door, visitors have to park 70 yards away in the lots that hold business vehicles during the day. It's advisable to wear street clothes or a cover unless you look forward to being ogled by the people working late nearby. Inside the unlabeled door, the small office can get crowded as people sign in (waivers required) and pay their tolls. It's reasonably priced and there's a discount if you are a member. I joined, even though I only make it to Dallas a few times a year, because I don't want to see the space close. Once guests are registered, a side door takes us into a social area where there are many places to sit, toys and artwork to look at or buy and, usually, the evening's smorgasbord, brought by the participants. There is usually porn playing on the TV, but very few people pay it much attention; everyone is busy talking to friends, hopefully gazing at strangers or preparing for what's to come.

A door in the back leads to the play space, which is subdivided into several areas. There is an open space sufficient to swing a twelve-foot whip, a dog cage and assorted other pieces of furniture. Off of that room are a small medical room, a classroom and a jail cell, each well-appointed for its purpose. Seating is limited in this area, but there's plenty of room to stand and watch.

Beyond this is the main dungeon. There are a few places for suspensions, racks, crosses, benches and sufficient other furniture to host 25 scenes at a time. The lighting is low in most spots, but there are a couple that have more illumination. The seating in the main room is generous and plush with chairs, couches and cushions scattered around the periphery. The entire vibe is well suited to sceneing.

Dungeon rules usually include no penetration or aerosolized blood, pre-notification of DMs (in red sashes) of any fire or heavy play, no food in the play areas without talking to a DM, etc. It's reasonably liberal with no unusual restrictions.

Having visited dungeons across the country, the Sanctuary compares very favorably. Its closest competition I've found so far is 1763 in Atlanta, which has certain advantages (review to follow), but, all in all, I'll take the Sanctuary any day.

Book Review

The Killer Wore Leather
By Laura Antoniou

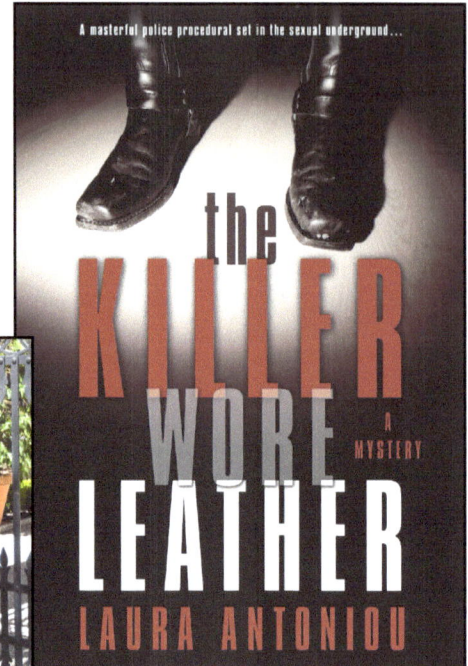

The Killer Wore Leather is Laura Antoniou's new murder mystery with a fictitious international leather competition, Mr. and Ms. Global Leather and Bootblack, as its backdrop. Think IML… no, don't think IML. Oh forget it; go ahead and think that, if you want, because this fictional competition is clearly a very thinly veiled replica of that alt-culture institution.

Once I got a few pages into the novel I knew I would have to invite Laura to be a guest on the Erotic Mind Show. (To find this podcast, visit *drdicksexadvice.com* and search for Laura Antoniou.) It was great getting to know Laura and hearing the whole delicious backstory dish on the novel. Laura is wickedly funny and astonishingly subversive. Interestingly enough, these are the very same characteristics that I liked most about the novel.

The Killer Wore Leather opens at the Grand Sterling Hotel, NYC. Thousands of people are arriving for the annual leather competition and fetish ball. Anyone who has ever attended one of these fêtes in real life will feel right at home. Most of the main characters and all of the supporting characters are right out of (fetish) central casting. There is even an Antoniou-esque, rabblerousing gadfly who makes regular appearances throughout the novel just to stir the shit. *So* unlike Ms. Antoniou, don'tcha know.

The reigning Mr. Global Leather, Mack Steel, who is also one of the contest judges, is the soon-to-be deceased. He is—how shall I put this—a real dick, and not in a good way. Just about everyone hates him, which will make for loads and loads of suspects once he is found murdered in his hotel room. Mr. Steel is stabbed to death with a trident-shaped weapon and left wearing only a pair of frilly knickers. Oh, the scandal!

Enter Detective Rebecca Feldblum and her new partner, Dominick DeCosta. Rebecca is a lipstick lesbian, and Dominick is a hot, straight, black guy. Both detectives are way out of their comfort zone surrounded by all the freaks. The convention promoters decide the show must go on, so despite the murder, Feldblum and DeCosta have to do their sleuthing amidst the fetish circus.

The Killer Wore Leather is a good, old-fashioned whodunit. And Antoniou lays on the detail; we are treated to a baffling array of characters from the sexual fringe and a barrage of alt-culture jargon. But don't let this deter you. The two detectives and another surprising character, a savvy newspaper reporter, act as a Greek chorus of sorts. Through them we are treated to a delightful exposé of some of the more fascinating nooks and crannies of the fetish and kink world. It's all great fun.

Antoniou's writing style is sharp, witty and smart. She lovingly skewers everyone and everything. I hasten to emphasize the word "lovingly," because there are no cheap shots here. There's never any doubt that Laura loves this slice of life and those that inhabit it. Her portrayals are hilarious, but respectful. However, she makes no bones about the fact that some of the minorities within this minority are being marginalized, and sometimes that gets ugly. Discrimination is rife, even within the sexual underground.

The thing that struck me most about the book is, as I mentioned earlier, Laura's brilliantly seditious streak. She's well known for her biting essays on alt culture, sexual roles and gender politics. And I am delighted to say that her keen observations bleed—you should pardon the pun—into her narrative. I loved it!

Buy *The Killer Wore Leather* for the mystery story; stay with it for the subversion.

The Killer Wore Leather
By Laura Antoniou
Cleis Press, 2013
ISBN: 157344930X

By Staff Reviewer

Event Review

THE GWNN BASH
Austin, TX

GWNN is the oldest pansexual group in central Texas, having celebrated with its 20th anniversary BASH in mid July. GWNN's official documents identify its mission as being a group "that serves as a gateway to the alternative community. It is non-commercial, not-for-profit and dues-free. It exists to provide a positive and dynamic environment for people to meet others with a similar social interest in bondage, domination, submission, sadism, masochism and other erotic or related topics."

This year's BASH was a little odd in that there seemed to be a serious slant towards Leather, looking at the people that took the floor as speakers and presenters, despite the fact that GWNN claims to be a gateway to the entire kink subculture in the area. There were eleven speakers who were Leather-identified and six who were not. The keynote speech was given by Guy Baldwin, who is very well-known as a presenter in Leather circles. We're sure it

was a thought-provoking keynote address, but it leads us to wonder why no one could be found who was more representative of the full membership. To put the question in perspective: In 2012, Laura Antoniou was the keynote speaker. Maybe GWNN should identify as a gateway group to Austin's Leather scene.

The list of classes included eleven on general topics and one on a specifically Leather topic, which, to us, emphasizes the confusion we felt at the event. There was the usual mix of BDSM introductory classes, a couple of advanced topics such as wet cupping and fantasy rape and some less-common topics including littles and petplay. Though we were unable to attend all of the classes, the reports we heard from attendees were quite mixed. The presenters that came in from out of town seemed to fare much better than the local talent.

The vendors' area featured about fifteen stalls with the usual mix of leather goods, corsets, toys and books. One of the more unusual booths was for a local harness maker who had some items for ponies that we've seldom seen at events. The most inexplicable booth was the Violet Wand Store, which was totally devoid of violet wands. In fact, it was missing any electrical toys at all. Perhaps they read the writing on the wall and realized that the event was set up to make vending as difficult as possible. During the three-day event, there was vending only on one day. Booths opened at 8am while attendees were still in their rooms or having breakfast. Vending continued while classes were in session, so there was very little traffic, but they were required to close during the keynote speech. And the last hour required vendors to sell as they packed, as everyone had to be out of the hall by 5pm. Many vendors were dissatisfied with the relatively high booth fee, considering the small number of attendees. We heard them calculate that there were only 2.5 hours of actual vending. More than one said that they do not plan to return to the BASH in the future unless it is made more vendor-friendly.

All of that being said, it did seem like a positive environment for the attendees, the vast majority of whom were local. GWNN seems to want to turn the BASH into a larger event that will appeal to a regional audience, but the secret to making that leap seems to elude them. This year's attempt to appeal to the local gay Leather community was unsuccessful in spite of special measures being taken, such as bringing in Guy Baldwin and making Keynote-Only tickets available. Until GWNN can find a way to include the people in their own city, it seems unlikely that they will be able to create an event that will inspire people to come from farther than Dallas or Houston. This year's BASH seemed a somewhat desperate attempt to appear more significant than it was.

––––––––––––––

Rating the BASH

In order to better serve our readers, our staff reviews events all over the US and Canada. We have devised a rating system, albeit imperfect, which reflects our opinions of the events listed below. If we have incorrect information, please write us and let us know.

Profile:

Name of event, sponsor, contact information (web site): GWNN BASH XX

Type of Event: We're having trouble classifying the BASH. It didn't seem to know what it was.

S – Designed for a primarily straight audience

L – Designed for a Leather audience

M – Designed for a pansexual audience

Size: A (A – Small; 0 – 200 paid attendees)

Program: K, P, V, & X

K – Has a key note speaker

P – Has Presentations and classes

V – Has Vendors

X – Has Special Interest components (Puppy/Pony/ Little space, Competitions, etc...)

Power Exchange Rating: 2

2 – Event on the fade; smaller and less important each year

If your event is not listed or rated, please contact us and invite one of our reviewers to attend. A featured review and listing will follow.

PEM Guide to the Best presenters

If you see any of these presenters on an event schedule your should make an effort to hear them. We think they are among the best there are.

Anne Bryne

Anne has been involved in the fetish scene far longer than she cares to admit. Through her activities as a long time vendor at many local and national events, she has had the opportunity to meet, listen and learn from the best of our community. She credits her first interest in Violet Wands to a chance encounter with Lady Velvet, who did much to promote and share her knowledge of violet wands throughout the country. This led to the happy pairing with her business partner Doug, the engineer who breathes life into her ideas.

Slave Caroline

slave Caroline has been "kinky" since her earliest memory. Since her late teens she has served a number of Masters with different genders and sexual orientations in one form of Ds or Ms relationship. Along with a lifetime interest in spirituality, meditation, theology, and philosophy, her journey in slavery has been her central path to the sacred through love, devotion, surrender, service, and authority exchange. She is a clinical, depth, liberation psychologist, philosopher, businesswoman, a spiritual seeker/teacher as well as a deep lifestyle slave.

Scott Smith

With his creative and rather deviant mind, Scott Smith enthusiastically developed his techniques of bondage and suspension from his experience with nautical and high angle rope work. The powerful physical interactions that became the hallmark of his S&M activities were initially necessities for various activities including white water rafting, scuba, climbing, and paramedical rescue.

Skip Chasey

Skip Chasey, a/k/a Master Skip, heads a family of spiritually grounded leatherfolk in the City of Angels, where he is a practicing spiritual director and certified Grief Recovery™ counselor and also earns a living as a missionary among the savages of Hollywood. As an out and proud leatherman, Master Skip addressed a crowd of nearly one million people at the Millennium March on Washington, and since then he has given a dozen keynote addresses and presented over 200 programs on the spiritual dynamics of SM and D/s relationships at noteworthy leather events throughout the US and Canada.

Bendyogagirl

Bendy Yoga Girl has been teaching and training groups and individuals for almost 30 years. She has been actively exploring D/s and authority exchange for over 25 years, and she has a long history with BDSM. While her proclivities tend towards authority exchange and spiritual awakening through kink over all else, she is a lover of rope, deep impact, sensation, takedowns, and having fun!

Kristen Knapic

Kristen Knapick, MA, LMHCA, is a psychotherapist in private practice in Seattle. She specializes in working with those for whom kink/poly/sex work/queerness/ gender variance are a part of life, whether the source of a problem or not. Her nearly twenty years of experience as a member of all of these communities give her a unique, nonjudgmental perspective on mental health within them, and her professional training has sharpened her skills. Kristen has presented at Babeland, Powersurge, Living in Leather, the Center for Sex Positive Culture, Women

in Kink, and Gender Odyssey. She has organized professional trainings for mental health providers on polyamory and BDSM.

Bondage Lessons Max

Max has been active in Seattle's kink community since 1992 and has been teaching bondage, BDSM, and polyamory workshops since 1999. He's actively and successfully polyamorous and has several wonderful long-term partners. While he is proficient with a wide range of BDSM skills, Max especially enjoys the intimacy of rope bondage. Max projects a gentle, dominant energy, and all of his relationships – and most of his scenes – include a substantial d/s component.

Dr. Robert Rubel

Robert Rubel (Dr. Bob), is an educational sociologist and researcher by training. He has ten books currently in print (four on Master/ slave topics, two on advanced sex techniques, one on fire play, and three erotic art photo books). Recipient of the 2008 Pantheon of Leather's Community Choice Award, Robert has been involved in the BDSM scene since the summer of 2001, throwing himself into the literature of the field as though it were an academic study.

Robert Ritchey

Master/slave relations; basic rope and fire play.

Since 2003, Bob has been learning to embrace his love of rope bondage for its aesthetic as well as other appeals. Mixing that with his love of teaching has had him presenting to mainstream and kinky audiences ever since. He has been the Education Coordinator for the School for Austin Area D/s Education twice, created a local group to provide information to people new to kink to enable them to avoid the pitfalls that trip up so many. One thing he has learned is that every time he teach, he says that he learns something new. He is now traveling the world to learn what he can from alternative voices from all corners of the globe.

Laura Antoniou

Laura Antoniou is the author of the well-known *Marketplace* series of erotic novels. Her work has been translated into Spanish, German, Hebrew, Japanese and Korean. Laura won the prestigious John Preston Short Fiction Award from the National Leather Association in both 2011 and in 2012. In 2013, Laura published her first mystery, The Killer Wore Leather, a murder mystery that takes place at a leather contest.

As a presenter, panelist, and keynote speaker, Laura has appeared at dozens of conferences over more than twenty years, both entertaining and delivering an occasional verbal indictment. She has also appeared at colleges and universities, including Harvard, NYU, Rutgers, Columbia and the University of Washington. She received the NLA: International's Lifetime Achievement Award in 2011.

Richard Wagner

Richard Wagner, M.Div., Ph.D., ACS, is a psychotherapist and clinical sexologist in private practice in Seattle.

Richard has been a practitioner of sex therapy and relationship counseling for over thirty years. He has also been involved in all sorts of sex-education and sexual-enrichment projects. One such outlet is his online sex advice column, which he's been writing for well over fifteen years. During that time it's been syndicated on a number of sites. Now his column and weekly podcasts have a home of their own: drdicksexadvice.com. He also contributes to several other websites as a guest columnist.

He is renowned for his long- and short-term seminars and workshops for healing and helping professionals, sexual minorities, men living with and through prostate cancer, and women and men affected by sex abuse and sexual trauma.

He often speaks in the public forum on policy issues related to religion, human sexuality, aging, death and dying, and the clergy sex-abuse scandal.

Power Exchange Magazine's Bookshelf

Recommended Reading

Books if you're just starting out in BDSM

The Gospel of Kink: A Modern Guide To Asking For What You Want And Getting What You Ask For by Richard Wagner, M. Div., Ph.D., ACS
> A workbook designed for forming, building and deepening alt culture relationships through effective communication.

The Ultimate Guide to Kink: BDSM, Role Play and the Erotic Edge
by Tristan Taormino
> The first major guide to BDSM in a generation—a bold and sexy collection of essays that run the gamut from expert how-to tutorials to provocative essays that delve into complex questions about desire, power, and pleasure.

Screw the Roses, Send Me the Thorns: The Romance and Sexual Sorcery of Sadomasochism by Philip Miller and Molly Devon
> The classic guide to sadomasochism that is intended to strip away myth, shame and fear, about BDSM to reveal truths about this intense form of eroticism.

When Someone You Love is Kinky by Dossie Easton and Catherine Liszt
> Very helpful for explaining your interest and involvement in BDSM to non-kinky family and friends.

Sensuous Magic, 2ⁿᵈ Edition: A Guide to S/M for Adventurous Couples
by Patick Califia

> Mixes erotic vignettes with practical advice and personal insights to produce a very creative guide to sadomasochism for couples.

SM 101: A Realistic Introduction by Jay Wiseman

> Thorough discussion of safety issues for most SM activities you'll experience. This is the "Bible" for SM play.

My Mentor, My Guide: A Handbook for Daddies and Boys for the New Generation
by Blade Bannon

> Offers you a new view on where our culture is heading and to offer a map to help navigate through treacherous waters as safely as possible.

Playing Well with Others by Lee Harrington and Mollena Williams

> The first book that explains kink culture that turn BDSM and leather from a bedroom predilection to a lifestyle and a community.

Books on the Psychological Aspects of BDSM

The New Topping Book by Janet W. Hardy and Dossie Easton

> Helps to explain what make someone a "good" dominant, including some of the mental aspects of being a dominant, offers some advice on BDSM plan and techniques, and covers the all important area of safety.

The New Bottoming Book by Janet W. Hardy and Dossie Easton

> The "mate" to the previously recommended book, this one is written for submissives/bottoms and deals largely with the mental/emotional aspects of being a submissive, rather than hands-on instructions in techniques and toys.

Partners in Power: Living in Kinky Relationships by Jack Rinella

> Answers the question: "Is it possible to form lasting, healthy, loving relationships that are based on power, control and pain?

The Control Book by Peter Masters

> About the fine art of taking control of your partner – the processes involved, using control, ensuring that you have control, and – importantly – about giving control back once you are done with it. To his vast credit, Masters also discusses how to fix a situation if it goes psychologically wrong.

This Curious Human Phenomenon: An Exploration of Some Uncommonly Explored Aspects of BDSM by Peter Masters

> There is material in this book that you simply won't find addressed by any other author.

Handbook of Erotic Dominance by Jack Rinella

> Read particularly starting down the "Master/slave" path.

Core Readings for Master/slave

Ask the Man Who Owns Him: The real lives of gay Masters and slaves by David Stein with David Schachter

> Interviews with long-term gay Master/slave couples: demonstrates the wide variety of approaches to hierarchical relationship structures.

Leading and Supportive Love: The Truth About Dominant and Submissive Relationships by Chris M. Lyon

> Describes workable ways to establish and maintain hierarchical relationships that are mutually supportive.

Master/slave Relations: Handbook of Theory and Practice by Robert J Rubel

> This will provide your best opportunity to get an overall understanding of Master/slave relationships – especially about things to think about before starting one and techniques for maintaining such a structure once you're in one.

SlaveCraft: Roadmaps for Erotic Servitude – Principles, Skills and Tools by Guy Baldwin

> Profound and masterful book discussing the philosophy and practice of service.)

Protocol Handbook for the Female slave: Handbook of Theory and Practice
by Robert J. Rubel

> An actual slave's protocol manual, this gives ample examples of protocols that can be modified for your particular relationship.

Master/slave Relations: Communications 401 – the advanced course
by Robert J. Rubel

> Out-of-the-box communications book that provides a wide range of work-arounds to often-hidden communication challenges.

Books about the Leather Culture

Urban Aboriginals by Geoff Mains

> This book explores the spiritual, sexual, emotional, cultural, and physiological aspects that make this "scene" one of the most prominent yet misunderstood subcultures in our society.

Kink And The City: An Englishman in New York by John Smith

> Taking us on a very real voyage of discovery though the subculture of kink in Gotham, the author opens each new door with trepidation and holds it open for the reader to experience every new encounter, each more outrageous than the next.

Leathersex: A Guide for the Curious Outsider and the Serious Player by Joseph Bean

> Another of the basic books about Leather by one of the most knowledgeable and lucid writers to tackle the topic.

Ties that Bind: The SM/Leather/Fetish Erotic Style: Issues, Commentaries and Advice by Guy Baldwin

> A practicing psychologist and one of the most important thinkers on subjects of SM/leather/fetish erotic style covering relationship issues, the Leather community, the SM experience, and personal transformation, as they relate to this form of erotic play.

<u>The Leatherman's Handbook</u> by Larry Townsend

> First book to write out the codes of conduct that the underground Leather scene and SM play that gay Leathermen lived by.

Books about Leather Spirituality

<u>Sacred Kink: The Eightfold Paths Of BDSM And Beyond</u> by Lee Harrington

> Modern tools of BDSM, fetish, kink and erotic adventuring have roots that go far back into history, tools that have been used for reaching altered states of consciousness, creating spiritual epiphanies, and changing lives.

<u>Soul of a Second Skin: The Journey of a Gay Christian Leatherman</u> by Hardy Haberman

> Nationally known and respected leatherman, author and speaker reveals his spiritual journey and gives readers both kinky and straight insight into the soul.

Erotica

<u>Hidden Agenda – Book One in The Perfect Submissive Trilogy</u> by Kay Jaybee

> If you like to read ultra-kinky, smart erotica, then this book's for you.

<u>The Voyeur</u> by Kay Jaybee

> Imaginative, kinky, sexy and keeps you guessing throughout. A well written, BDSM packed novel with lots of straight and lesbian sex.

<u>Under Her Thumb: Erotic Stories of Female Domination</u> By DL King

> Will whet your appetite for all things Fem Dom

<u>Surrender: Erotic Tales of Female Pleasure and Submission</u> by Donna George Storey

> Submissive women and dominant men showcase their fantasies, desires, and deepest wishes.

event listings

Albany Bound

Albany, NY   *Dates:* TBA   www.albanybound.com

Presentation: Yes   *Vendors:* Yes   *Contests:* No

Special Notes: Gay, Leather

All Male – Black Leather BDSM Party

Black River Falls, WI   *Dates:* TBA   www.campncn.com

Presentation: Yes   *Vendors:* Yes   *Contests:* No

Special Notes: Gay, Leather

Beat Me in St. Louis

St. Louis, MO   *Dates:* March 28-30, 2014   www.stl3.com

Presentation: Yes   *Vendors:* Yes   *Contests:* No

Special Notes: N/A

GWNN BASH

Austin, TX   *Dates:* TBA   www.gwnn.net/Bash2013/Intro

Presentation: Yes   *Vendors:* Yes   *Contests:* No

Special Notes: N/A

Beltane Gathering

Darlington, MD   *Dates:* May 2014   www.turtlehillevents.org/beltane

Presentation: Yes   *Vendors:* Yes   *Contests:* No

Special Notes: Camping, Sacred Sexuality, Pagan

Beyond Leather

Ft. Lauderdale, FL   *Dates:* May 1-4, 2014   www.beyondleather.net

Presentation: Yes   *Vendors:* Yes   *Contests:* Yes

Special Notes: Leather, Pony Play, Contests – International Power Exchange, International Pony Play Championship

event listings

Beyond Vanilla

Dallas, TX

Dates: September 27-29, 2013

www.beyondvanilla.org

Presentation: Yes

Vendors: Yes

Contests: No

Special Notes: N/A

Bizarre Bazaar

Panorama City, CA

Dates: November 2013

www.bizarrebazaar.org

Presentation: Yes

Vendors: Yes

Contests: No

Special Notes: N/A

Black BEAT

Baltimore, MD

Dates: TBA

www.blackbeatinc.org

Presentation: Yes

Vendors: Yes

Contests: No

Special Notes: Black

BOLD Con

Los Angeles, CA

Dates: February 21-23, 2014

www.boldcon.com

Presentation: Yes

Vendors: No

Contests: No

Special Notes: MDHL-fs (Male Dominant Heterosexual Leather – female submissive)

Bondage Expo Dallas

Dallas, TX

Dates: TBA

www.bondageexpodallas.com

Presentation: Yes

Vendors: Yes

Contests: No

Special Notes: Bondage

Boot Camp

Darlington, MD

Dates: TBA

www.northerndelawareds.com/boot-camp

Presentation: Yes

Vendors: Yes

Contests: No

Special Notes: Camping

event listings

Bound in Boston

Norwood, MA

Dates: October 5-6, 2013

www.boundinboston.com

Presentation: Yes

Vendors: No

Contests: No

Special Notes: Bondage

Brimstone

Asbury Park, NJ

Dates: November 28 – December 1, 2013

www.brimstonenj.com

Presentation: Yes

Vendors: No

Contests: No

Special Notes: Bondage

Burning Man

Black Rock City, NV

Dates: August 25 – September 1, 2014

www.burningman.com

Presentation: Yes

Vendors: No

Contests: No

Special Notes: Burner

Camp Crucible

Darlington, MD

Dates: May 24 – June 1, 2014

www.campcrucible.com

Presentation: Yes

Vendors: Yes

Contests: No

Special Notes: Camping

Camp NCN Spank

Black River Falls, WI

Dates: TBA

www.campncn.com

Presentation: Yes

Vendors: Yes

Contests: No

Special Notes: Camping

Charm City Fetish Fair

Baltimore, MD

Dates: TBA

www.charmcityfetishfair.com

Presentation: Yes

Vendors: Yes

Contests: No

Special Notes: N/A

event listings

CLAW

Cleveland, OH   *Dates:* April 24-27, 2014   www.clawinfo.org

Presentation: Yes   *Vendors:* Yes   *Contests:* No

Special Notes: Gay, Leather

COPE

Columbus, OH   *Dates:* September 13-14, 2013   www.adventuresinsexuality.org/COPE.html

Presentation: Yes   *Vendors:* Yes   *Contests:* No

Special Notes: N/A

Dark Odyssey

Northern Maryland   *Dates:* September 11-16, 2013   www.darkodyssey.com

Presentation: Yes   *Vendors:* No   *Contests:* No

Special Notes: Camping

Dark Odyssey

San Francisco, CA   *Dates:* November 15-18, 2013   www.darkodyssey.com

Presentation: Yes   *Vendors:* Yes   *Contests:* Yes

Special Notes: Contest – Little Miss Littles SF

Debauchery

Greensboro, NC   *Dates:* TBA   www.debaucherync.com

Presentation: Yes   *Vendors:* Yes   *Contests:* No

Special Notes: N/A

DomCon – ATL

Atlanta, GA   *Dates:* October 17-20, 2013   www.domconatlanta.com

Presentation: Yes   *Vendors:* Yes   *Contests:* Yes

Special Notes: Contests – Pantheon of Leather, Southeast Olympus Leather

event listings

DomCon – LA

Los Angeles, CA | Dates: TBA | www.domconla.com
Presentation: Yes | Vendors: Yes | Contests: Yes
Special Notes: Contest – Olympus Leather

FetFest

Aberdeen, MD | Dates: TBA | www.fetfest.com
Presentation: Yes | Vendors: Yes | Contests: No
Special Notes: N/A

Fetish Con

Tampa, FL | Dates: TBA | www.fetishcon.com
Presentation: Yes | Vendors: Yes | Contests: No
Special Notes: Trade Show

Fetish Fair Fleamarket

Warwick, RI | Dates: March 7-9, 2014 | www.fetishfairfleamarket.com
Presentation: Yes | Vendors: Yes | Contests: No
Special Notes: N/A

Floating World

Edison, NJ | Dates: TBA | www.thefloatingworld.org
Presentation: Yes | Vendors: Yes | Contests: No
Special Notes: N/A

Folsom Street Fair

San Francisco, CA | Dates: September 29, 2013 | www.folsomstreetfair.com
Presentation: Yes | Vendors: Yes | Contests: No
Special Notes: N/A

event listings

Folsom Fringe

San Francisco, CA   *Dates:* September 27-29, 2013   www.folsomfringe.com

Presentation: Yes   *Vendors:* Yes   *Contests:* No

Special Notes: N/A

Frolicon

Atlanta, GA   *Dates:* April 17-20, 2014   www.frolicon.com

Presentation: Yes   *Vendors:* Yes   *Contests:* No

Special Notes: N/A

GLLA Weekend

Indianapolis, IN   *Dates:* TBA   www.greatlakesleather.org

Presentation: Yes   *Vendors:* Yes   *Contests:* Yes

Special Notes: Contests – Bootblack, Master/slave, Ms. Leather Pride, Sir/boy

---

International Mr. Leather

Chicago, IL   *Dates:* May 23-26, 2014   www.imrl.com

Presentation: No   *Vendors:* Yes   *Contests:* Yes

Special Notes: Contests – Bootblack, Master/slave, Ms. Leather Pride, Sir/boy

---

International Ms. Leather

San Francisco, CA   *Dates:* April 18-21, 2014   www.imsl.org

Presentation: Yes   *Vendors:* Yes   *Contests:* Yes

Special Notes: Contests – International Ms. Leather, International Ms. Bootblack

---

Kinko De Mayo

Cleveland, OH   *Dates:* May 2-4, 2014   www.kinkodemayo.com

Presentation: Yes   *Vendors:* Yes   *Contests:* No

Special Notes: N/A

---

event listings

KinkFest

Portland, OR	*Dates:* March 21-23, 2014	www.kinkfest.org
Presentation: Yes	*Vendors:* Yes	*Contests:* No
Special Notes: N/A		

Kinky Karnival

Wichita, KS	*Dates:* June 2014	www.kinkykarnivalks.com
Presentation: Yes	*Vendors:* Yes	*Contests:* No
Special Notes: N/A		

Kinky Kollege

Chicago, Il	*Dates:* October 18-20 2013	www.kinkykollege.com
Presentation: Yes	*Vendors:* Yes	*Contests:* No
Special Notes: N/A		

Leather History Conference

Winston-Salem, NC	*Dates:* October 25-27, 2013	www.leatherhistoryconference.com
Presentation: Yes	*Vendors:* Yes	*Contests:* No
Special Notes: N/A		

Leather Leadership Conference

Philadelphia, PA	*Dates:* April 11-13. 2014	www.leatherleadership.org
Presentation: Yes	*Vendors:* Yes	*Contests:* No
Special Notes: N/A		

Leather & Leis

Maui, HI	*Dates:* March 4-8, 2014	www.leatherandleis.com
Presentation: Yes	*Vendors:* Yes	*Contests:* Yes
Special Notes: Contests – The Queen's Cup International Pony Competition		

event listings

Leather Flea and Play

Washington, DC   *Dates:* October 26, 2013   www.the-crucible.com/lfandp27.htm

Presentation: Yes   *Vendors:* Yes   *Contests:* No

Special Notes: N/A

Let Us Entertain You

Houston, TX   *Dates:* March 6-9, 2014   www.lueyweekend.com

Presentation: Yes   *Vendors:* Yes   *Contests:* Yes

Special Notes: Contests – TFL Hat Contest

MadtownKinkfest

Madison, WI   *Dates:* January 31-February 2, 2014   www.madtownkinkfest.com

Presentation: Yes   *Vendors:* Yes   *Contests:* No

Special Notes: Contest – Fetish Pageant

Master/slave Conference

Rockville, MD   *Dates:* TBA   www.masterslaveconference.org

Presentation: Yes   *Vendors:* Yes   *Contests:* Yes

Special Notes: Contests – Northeast Master/slave

Mid-Atlantic Leather Weekend

Washington, DC   *Dates:* January 17-20, 2014   www.leatherweekend.com

Presentation: No   *Vendors:* Yes   *Contests:* Yes

Special Notes: Contest – Mr. Mid-Atlantic Leather

Mischief in May

Des Moines, IA   *Dates:* May 16-18, 2014   www.mischiefinmay.com

Presentation: Yes   *Vendors:* Yes   *Contests:* No

Special Notes: N/A

event listings

Northeast Leather Weekend

Providence, RI | *Dates:* April 4-6, 2014 | www.northeastleather.com/weekend.html

Presentation: No | *Vendors:* Yes | *Contests:* Yes

Special Notes: Contests – Northeast Leather Sir, Leather boy, Leather Woman, Community Bootblack

---

Northwest Leather Celebration

San Jose/Silicon Valley, CA | *Dates:* May 16-18, 2014 | www.northwestleathercelebration.com

Presentation: Yes | *Vendors:* Yes | *Contests:* Yes

Special Notes: Contest – Northwest Master/slave

Northern Exposure

Anchorage, AK | *Dates:* TBA | www.northernexposurealaska.com

Presentation: Yes | *Vendors:* Yes | *Contests:* No

Special Notes: N/A

Paradise Unbound

Seattle, WA | *Dates:* August 5-10, 2014 | www.paradiseunbound.com

Presentation: Yes | *Vendors:* Yes | *Contests:* No

Special Notes: Camping

Pony and Critter Jamboree

Los Angeles, CA | *Dates:* TBA | www.laponiesandcritters.com

Presentation: Yes | *Vendors:* Yes | *Contests:* Yes

Special Notes: Pony/Critter Play

Power Exchange Summit

Columbus, OH | *Dates:* May 30-June 1, 2014 | www.powerexchangesummit.org

Presentation: Yes | *Vendors:* Yes | *Contests:* No

Special Notes: N/A

---

event listings

Rochester Erotic Arts Feastival

Rochester, NY   *Dates:* April 2014   www.rochestereroticartfest.org

Presentation: Yes   *Vendors:* Yes   *Contests:* No

Special Notes: Contest – Cat Walk, Erotic Tattoo

Rope Camp

Darlington, MD   *Dates:* July 9-13, 2014   www.turtlehillevents.org/theropecamp

Presentation: Yes   *Vendors:* Yes   *Contests:* No

Special Notes: Camping

Rubber Doll World Rendezvous

Minneapolis, MN   *Dates:* June 2014   www.rubberdollworldrendezvous.com

Presentation: Yes   *Vendors:* Yes   *Contests:* No

Special Notes: Rubber/Latex

Sin in the City

Las Vegas, NV   *Dates:* February 28-March 2, 2014   www.sin-in-the-city.com

Presentation: Yes   *Vendors:* Yes   *Contests:* Yes

Special Notes: Contest – Southwest Olympus Leather

Shibaricon

Chicago, Il   *Dates:* May 23-26, 2014   www.shibaricon.com

Presentation: Yes   *Vendors:* Yes   *Contests:* No

Special Notes: Bondage

Smokeout

Las Vegas, NV   *Dates:* TBA   www.lasvegassmokeout.com

Presentation: No   *Vendors:* No   *Contests:* No

Special Notes: Gay, Tobacco

event listings

Snowbound Leather Weekend

Provincetown, MA *Dates:* February 21-23, 2014 www.matesleatherweekend.com/snowbound

Presentation: Yes *Vendors:* Yes *Contests:* Yes

Special Notes: Contest – Mr. Snowbound

South Plains Leather Fest

Dallas, TX *Dates:* March 7-9, 2014 www.southplainsleatherfest.com

Presentation: Yes *Vendors:* Yes *Contests:* Yes

Special Notes: Contest – International Master/slave

SouthEast LeatherFest

Atlanta, GA *Dates:* June 19-22, 2014 http://secure.seleatherfest.com

Presentation: Yes *Vendors:* Yes *Contests:* Yes

Special Notes: Contest – SouthEast Master/slave, boy, Bootblack, Mr./Ms. SouthEast LeatherFest

Southwest Leather Conference

Phoenix, AZ *Dates:* January 23-26, 2014 www.southwestleather.org

Presentation: Yes *Vendors:* Yes *Contests:* Yes

Special Notes: Contest – Southwest Master/slave, Bootblack

Spanksgiving

St. Louis, MO *Dates:* November 22-24, 2013 http://2013.spanksgiving-stl.com

Presentation: Yes *Vendors:* Yes *Contests:* No

Special Notes: N/A

Spring Iniquity

Houston, TX *Dates:* TBA www.nlahoustontx.org/iniquity/default.html

Presentation: No *Vendors:* No *Contests:* No

Special Notes: Contest – Mr. Prime Choice. Bar Run

event listings

TES FEST
Piscataway, NJ | *Dates:* TBA | www.tesfest.org
Presentation: Yes | *Vendors:* Yes | *Contests:* No
Special Notes: N/A

Thunder in the Mountains
Denver, CO | *Dates:* July 11-13, 2014 | www.thunderinthemountains.com
Presentation: Yes | *Vendors:* Yes | *Contests:* No
Special Notes: N/A

Tribal Fire
Oklahoma City, OK | *Dates:* May 2-4, 2014 | www.tribalfireokc.com
Presentation: Yes | *Vendors:* Yes | *Contests:* No
Special Notes: N/A

Twisted Tryst
Indiana/Wisconsin | *Dates:* June/August 2014 | www.twistedtryst.com
Presentation: Yes | *Vendors:* Yes | *Contests:* No
Special Notes: Camping

Up Your Alley
San Francisco, CA | *Dates:* July 27, 2014 | www.folsomstreetfair.com/alley
Presentation: Yes | *Vendors:* Yes | *Contests:* No
Special Notes: N/A

Winter Wickedness
Columbus, OH | *Dates:* February 7-9, 2014 | www.adventuresinsexuality.org
Presentation: Yes | *Vendors:* Yes | *Contests:* No
Special Notes: N/A

event listings

Women's International Leatherfest

Dallas, TX   *Dates:* TBA   www.wilfest.net

Presentation: Yes   *Vendors:* Yes   *Contests:* Yes

Special Notes: Contest – Women's International Leather Legacy

Canada

Lupercalia

Edmonton, AB   *Dates:* February 14-16, 2014   www.lupercalia-edmonton.org

Presentation: Yes   *Vendors:* Yes   *Contests:* No

Special Notes: N/A

Montreal Fetish Weekend

Montreal, QC   *Dates:* TBA   www.fetishweekend.com

Presentation: Yes   *Vendors:* Yes   *Contests:* No

Special Notes: N/A

Rubbout

Vancouver, BC   *Dates:* TBA   www.rubbout.com

Presentation: Yes   *Vendors:* Yes   *Contests:* No

Special Notes: Gay, Rubber

Tease

Bayham, ON   *Dates:* July 10-14, 2014   www.get-teased.ca

Presentation: Yes   *Vendors:* Yes   *Contests:* No

Special Notes: Camping

event listings

WestCoast Bound

Vancouver, BC   *Dates:* February 7-9, 2014   www.westcoastbound.ca

Presentation: Yes   *Vendors:* Yes   *Contests:* No

Special Notes: N/A

Europe

German Fetish Ball

Berlin, DE   *Dates:* TBA   www.german-fetish-ball.com

Presentation: Yes   *Vendors:* Yes   *Contests:* No

Special Notes: N/A

London Fetish Fair

London, UK   *Dates:* 2nd Sundays   www.londonfetishfair.co.uk

Presentation: Yes   *Vendors:* Yes   *Contests:* No

Special Notes: N/A

Power Exchange Magazine has attempted to accumulate an accurate listing of events for the purpose of evaluating and letting our readers know our recommendation for attendance. If you see an error or omission or want to add to the listing, please contact us at editor@powerexchangemagazine.com. The staff evaluations and recommendations will appear next issue.

www.ingramcontent.com/pod-product-compliance
Lightning Source LLC
LaVergne TN
LVHW072108070426
835509LV00002B/65

*9 7 8 1 6 1 0 9 8 3 6 6 2 *